WHO IS MARY SUE?

SOPHIE COLLINS

Who Is Mary Sue?

FABER & FABER

First published in 2018
by Faber & Faber Ltd
Bloomsbury House
74–77 Great Russell Street
London WC1B 3DA

Typeset by Hamish Ironside
Printed in England by Martins the Printers, Berwick-upon-Tweed

A CIP record for this book is available from the British Library

ISBN 978-0-571-34661-5

2 4 6 8 10 9 7 5 3 1

Contents

WHO IS MARY SUE?

I'll never finish lifting up these faces.
CLAUDE CAHUN

PREFACE

I recently read a novel that resisted a conventional representation of self. At the outset, the protagonist – whose name is mentioned just once in the book, in passing – travels abroad to teach on a short-term writing course. With little introspection or background provided on her part, reality is built primarily through others' life experiences (or what they choose to share of them) as filtered through the narrator's working memory and language.

These second-hand accounts fill the book in reams, beginning with the marital history of an older man – the narrator's neighbour on her outbound flight – and finishing up with the recent events in the life of another visiting writer. The latter, a playwright, tells the protagonist of her involvement in a violent mugging and the behavioural changes, including a fresh inability to self-express and a compulsive need to consume sugar, precipitated by trauma.

At the foot of these stories – at once ludicrously vague and full with detail – is a frayed hole, a conspicuous lack of identity in the very place that has most often been tasked with generating readerly incentive.

Threadworms, stray hairs: loose threads surround the hole, invading it. They are disturbing: they are unruly, and they emphasise a persisting absence.

In another book, a non-fiction, the same author recognises the ice cream parlour as a place in which personal identities are sometimes fleshed out. Here, she writes, children are generally happy to select the familiar flavours, whereas adults often experience an anxiety of self-presentation: *the fear of misrepresenting their own ideas.*

We say we love each other but we eat each other up.

Dear No. 24601

The future is an eye that I don't dare look into
Last night I dreamed I was a ball of fire
and woke up on the wrong side of the room
this is a recurring dream
I share an apartment with my twin sister
Enclosed is a photo of us on a tandem bike
I forget which one I am
Sometimes I wake up believing I am her
she is me
and there is nothing about the day to indicate otherwise
Weeks stack up this way
As a girl I did not do well with other children
Unable to see the fun in games
which were only ever maddening
I paid close attention to the weather
delighting in hail and not much else
save a prized collection of Hummel figurines
derived from the pastoral sketches
of Sister Maria Innocentia Hummel
German Franciscan nun and talented artist
Her simple peaceful works
drew the enduring hatred of Hitler himself
You know Hummel translates as 'bumblebee' in German
and they say she was always 'buzzing around'
What do you think do we grow into our names
or does kismet know a thing
One name can mean too much
the other not nearly enough
The details make a difference
like sitting on the white cushion

as opposed to the blue
white is pure of course
but my soul's been in the bargain bin since Russia
and Lenin's tomb
I had a moment there
among the balustrades
and once that moment had expired
it graduated
from a moment to a life

Beauty Milk

I don't matter.
I am a blemish,
a fragment,
an apartment.

I am a multiplication
and a made-up belief.
I am nothing for days afterwards.

They say 'sum' about me
because they believe I am expanding.
Really I'm too clean cut.

This one time I was owned
but he wouldn't pay the charges
at the German border.

Russia is the pits.

Sister

Sister, listen to me – tonight our father will pull open the heavy door of our home, walk with his large boots into the kitchen and drop a pig on the table. In the morning, peasants with children and glassy-eyed babies will enter, sniffing at us like animals, noting the absence of a mother who lays out cold plates, white bread.

Healers

I encountered a scaffold
outside the Holy Trinity Church in Vladimir.
At first I didn't notice her
slumped against the side of the church –
she was pretty small for a scaffold, pretty un-
assuming. Her safety mesh
was torn in places and sun-bleached all over
and threatened to dislodge
due to a forceful wind that was typical
of the season. She was shaking.
She was fundamentally insecure.
She told me that good foundations are essential
but the men who had put her together
hadn't taken advantage of the right opportunities.
Now, each day, someone came by
called her 'unsafe' and also 'a liability'
then left, failing to initiate the dismantling process
that yes would have been painful
and slow, but kinder.
International visitors to the church
blamed her for the mess of tools and rags
on the grounds and for the fact
that they could no longer see
the church's celebrated mural
depicting Saint Artemy of Verkola
unusually pious
highly venerated
child saint killed by lightning.
His dead body radiated light
never showed signs of decay

and was in fact said to have effected
multiple miracles of healing.
I said comforting things to the scaffold
but she only seemed to lean more heavily
against the side of the church.
We are rarely independent structures she said
before she dropped a bolt pin
which released a long section of tube
which released another bolt pin
which released several wooden boards
which scraped another tube
and made an unbearable sound.

Eight Phrases

– My drink is getting lonely, would you like to join me with yours?

– What's your name?

– How long does the journey take?

– My father is a policeman.

– I do not have a brother.

– My birthday is January 8th.

– Your breath smells like peaches.

– Can you give me something for the pain?

WHO IS MARY SUE?

Coined by Paula Smith in 1973, 'Mary Sue' is a pejorative term used by writers and readers of fan fiction to describe protagonists who are believed to be thinly disguised versions of the fan fic author's idealised self.

There is no outright consensus as to Mary Sue's character type. Invariably, however,

Mary Sue is female;

she is said to be difficult to identify with, poorly constructed, without depth;

she is associated with narcissism and/or wish fulfilment.

I read that fear of creating a Mary Sue may be restricting and even silencing some writers.

'I don't know if I should be sending this to you,' wrote one young author in her cover letter to a magazine. 'I'm afraid it's a Mary Sue. Only I don't know what that is.'

On the iconic cover of her book *How to Suppress Women's Writing*, Joanna Russ lists, in a large, italicised, tangerine font, a set of common objections to female-authored works. Among them: '*She wrote it, but look what she wrote about.* (The bedroom, the kitchen, her family. Other women!)'; '*She wrote it, but she isn't really an artist, and it isn't really art.* (It's a thriller, a romance, a children's book. It's sci fi!)'.

Inside: 'men and women, whites and people of color do have very different experiences of life and one would expect such differences to be reflected in their art. I wish to emphasize here that I am not talking (vis-à-vis sex) about the relatively small area of biology . . . but about socially-enforced differences.'

Russ shares an anecdote. She is on a creative writing MA committee of three professors. The other two professors are male. The committee has the unenviable task of reading approximately two hundred manuscripts during the university's admissions period. In part one of the anecdote, Russ recalls disagreeing with her two male colleagues on the believability of a short story by a woman which ends with the female protagonist lying in bed next to her sleeping husband, wishing she had the courage to mutilate him with a piece of cooking equipment.

In part two, Russ remembers being impressed by a woman's poem in which a girl returning home from a date with a boy she does not like (throughout the evening the girl has had to 'work at it') opens the white refrigerator in her mother's kitchen to find that its interior is 'entirely covered with red cabbage roses'.

The male professors find the anger of the story's protagonist overstated, and the poem's essential image unrecognisable, disengaged.

Neither woman is admitted to the creative writing course.

Russ again: 'If women's experience is defined as inferior to, less important than, or "narrower" than men's experience, women's writing is automatically denigrated ... *She wrote it but look what she wrote about* becomes *She wrote it, but it's unintelligible/badly constructed/thin/spasmodic/uninteresting, etc.*, a statement by no means identical with *She wrote it, but I can't understand it* (in which case the failure might be with the reader).'

Thus Mary Sue becomes, in my eyes, an unwitting embodiment of the double standard of content.

I note that, in literary fiction, when a female writer's female protagonist *is* considered up to scratch, she is often taken to be a thinly disguised version of the author's *non*-idealised self.

Something like: a woman who tries to invent in literature will fail, whereas a woman who succeeds in writing is believed to have done so to the extent that she has been able to accurately portray the details of her own life.

She wrote it, but the protagonist's all her. (A Mary Sue!)

I begin to collect quotations, responses.

Among them:

INTERVIEWER

Could you say a little more about the relationship of your fictional characters to you, their author? The usual prurient question, about how autobiographical an author's fiction is, is especially tempting in your case . . .

LORRIE MOORE

Why is the usual prurient question especially tempting in my case? Is it really?

So, tell me, your new book, it features a woman who is from the islands, who has a husband who's a composer, they live in a North-eastern town, she has two kids – sounds a lot like you! How auto-biographical is it?

JAMAICA KINCAID

It's not about me but it's about things that I'm familiar with, and I hope a reader coming to it doesn't look for clues about anything that happened to me. It's about something deeper . . . My own self, my own everyday life is sort of very untidy and smelly, and kind of revolting, really.

Roland Barthes writes, 'Every biography is a novel that dares not speak its name.' Is the unnamed narrator of *nineties* actually called Lucy?

The narrator's name could be Lucy, but her name is certainly not 'Lucy Ives', or at any rate she isn't me . . . the narrator doesn't have a life in the same way that you or I do, which is of course obvious, but all the same I want to say that I don't intend for this narrator to have a life; I intend for her to tell this story.

SHARON OLDS

I would use the phrase *apparently personal poetry* for the kind of poetry that I think people are referring to as 'confessional'. *Apparently* personal because how do we really know? We don't.

The misuse of the term 'narcissism' in relation to my work is nauseating. My life is the trash going into the incinerator to power the book I'm trying to write.

THE ENGINE

I wrote the words 'I will be who'... That started something. I found myself writing and I couldn't stop. I realised, there's a whole story writing itself in my head and it's like a fable, an allegory of my life. I knew this was important.

BARBARA T. SMITH

I was able to fall asleep anywhere except in my own bed.

I experienced a persistent vice-like pain in my stomach, often followed by blood. I would usually take it upon myself to examine the blood, and the blood would usually contain sediment.

I became aware of visual irregularities in the inner-city air and understood them to be the physical manifestations of satellite signals. I attached great importance to the occasion of the manifestations' having revealed themselves to me, and referred to this event privately as the Faith Docking.

I had incestuous dreams about our father.

I learned the names of the Earth's artificial satellites and began to worship them as saints.

I had incestuous dreams.

On my walks I began to notice more bonfires than ever before. I was reluctant to speculate on a cause, but the hillside fields were plainly covered in scabs.

Horses roamed outside the stations like dogs and with the versatility of dogs. They maintained, however, a horse's incuriousness.

My only reading was of signs, but I read a lot of signs.

I began to recognise myself in glinting motes across the city's floors.

A theory about perennially leafless trees: they are petrified angels.

On a particular morning I woke with cold lips and nose, and the desire to bite down onto raw clay.

I thought again and again about the curdled smell and texture of disposable nappies, though I'd never touched one.

Outside, the heat carried itself in drifts. I noticed how the satellite signals would stick to the cold streams, whereas people tended to follow the warm.

I was halfway out on my walk to Minto before I remembered my birthday. I was standing in a field watching two identical piebald horses feed off the same bit of forage.

I thought I might be experiencing a medical emergency; I couldn't perceive any difference between the horses, and my boots were stuck to the ground.

I should have worn trousers; I got a tick, pulled it out wrong, and left its legs inside my leg.

I sat down, but instead of getting maudlin about it I decided to welcome it. I sang 'its legs inside my leg' to the tune of 'The Farmer in the Dell' for a few rounds, and picked at it for a while with a key without looking, quicker and harder as the nerves died off.

By the time I looked back at the wound it was awful, the size of a disc, and deep. I headed to the sea to wash it.

There was a stone on the beach, and the stone was important; when I picked it up I realised I could not go back to the city.

There were feathers on the beach, and the feathers were our father. I picked them up to make them part of my inventory. They smelled sweet, like airborne diseases.

Also in my inventory: a bottle opener, a menstrual cup, a lighter, a colouring book found at a bus stop, a cordless rape alarm.

The colouring book was esoteric. I could ask it questions and it would find a way to answer.

Example: I once asked the book whether I should enter a church that I had found. I closed my eyes and opened a page of the colouring book at random. It was the page that showed a chimney sweep doffing his hat. The doffing was a welcoming thing. It meant that I was welcome to explore the church.

While bathing in a creek I found a bag of ham, its plastic bowtie handles wedged under a rock. I broke into the bag, peeled off a small pink piece and put it in my mouth. The ham had the feel and taste of wet tissue paper. I spat it into the stream, even though I was starving, and discarded the bag.

I cried for myself as I watched the pink mush travel away on tiny bubbles of saliva.

I found an empty shed with unbroken windows. I counted myself lucky and lay down in the dog bed that was on the floor with a tarpaulin sheet for cover.

I fell into a heavy sleep and dreamed a procession of purebreeds: two Dalmatians, side by side; an Afghan hound; and some smaller ones, like a Shar-Pei with breathing problems (you could hear it in the panting).

When I woke from the dream there was a dog right over me, a mongrel with cataracts. The mongrel stayed looking for a moment before leaving, unhurried.

*
* *

Untitled

The village is always on fire.
Men stay away from the kitchens,
take up in outhouses with concrete floors,
while the women – soot in their hair –
initiate the flames into their small routines.

Before

In 1239 the Mongol leader Batu Khan led his hordes
in a full-scale invasion of Rus'
His chief khatun Borakchin meanwhile
was at home, knee-deep
in mutiny
The servants had
in the absence of the fearsome khan
begun to rebel in small but unacceptable ways
making eye contact
& addressing the khatun directly
representing just two misbehaviours
in this stream of noncompliance that culminated
in their spitting at her hair & body as she rose
from bed
They had always despised her shallow breathing (*Pretentiouùs!*)
the pale crown of her head
visible beneath an odd number of thin hairs (*Sick!*)
& permanently covered in beads of sweat, necessitating
the near-constant application
of some powder of dubious origin (*Abomïnable!*)
One late afternoon
after finding a pornographic etching on the inner lid
of her family box
Borakchin escaped the court unattended
to the North Gate
where she straddled an outsize stone turtle
& picked at the uneven skin surrounding her left thumbnail
wondering at the politics of transmission
until she became so furious that she began to resemble a little
     white monkey

What followed was a long period of rain
a yearning for empirical consequence
& an influx of anachronistic beetles
escaping time
Somewhere in the present
a table of sisters became silent the moment
their food was placed in front of them
Two trees were similar but not the same
they were sister trees
A Fiat Panda carrying a team of cleaners with dark hair
approached a Russian cathedral via a backroad
marked out by a low fence of dead reeds

As bread is the body of Christ
so is glass the very flesh of the Devil

I was beginning to worry our paperweights were not the best on the open market. Sales for us were steady, but for others sales were up. Our solid metal weights were elegant, but it was clear to me that the trend was towards glass in many shapes and colours, and with rare contours.

A faction of the community saw the Devil inside this kind of glass, and some inside glass in general. *As bread is the body of Christ so is glass the very flesh of the Devil*, and so they stuck to our copper, our brass. Besides which many of the older members simply found it difficult to get their heads around the material's technological aspects. 'I don't mind glass,' said Etel, for example, 'I just wish it would stop moving.'

Our company was called Knowing Roses, and we had existed for seven years. We had existed for seven years, an eternity, and now my life had some storm to it.

*
* *

It began at the idea of congruence. Congruence is the state achieved by coming together, the state of agreement. We are congruent when how we act and what we say is consistent with how we are feeling and what we are thinking. Even on a very simple level I have found that this statement seems to hold. For instance, it does not help for me to act as though I were well when in reality I am feeling quite ill.

The house was dim and very cold. I felt my nipples gone white, distended. They were incredibly painful, and I worried about a more permanent loss of sensation.

*
* *

Outside, on a patch of green grass they called 'English grass', I read the words of the book I had with me. They were the most important words to date. I knew this because after reading them, and quite suddenly, I felt my movements, my very countenance, corresponded to those I had previously coveted in other women, those that belonged to a kind of woman I knew (or thought I knew) I would never become.

I am not even pursing my lips now as I write this. And when I took my notebook from my rucksack just now my movements were studied. I know someone watches me (I watch myself). Perhaps this is the difference the words made.

Later, I climbed into bed, and shortly, of course, surely, it all went away, like the promise of a life, an embryo and its bedding.

The Palace of Culture and Science

No one has ever noted how milky it was
that no one could get milk
for not much
for a long time

I noticed men bending letters, repeating
my ideas

Just once I thought
I'd found acknowledgement
in the space between
two untranslatable words

left there by Irish monks

Poor Clare

On Sundays I wander the villa with the dog, and the other dogs.
They keep to themselves, incurious as horses. One of these days I
smell something, and in the smell I see a dead body, a plateau of
cloud, a saint.

At dinner that evening I read one section of my summary, 'The
Praise', aloud. It will be taken by a free periodical.

    One fat obscurity.

A week later Minoress calls me down to the forecourt. Halfway into
the interrogation I am made an orphan, a moment I've been halfway
in search of.

The weather makes me doubt myself: a vulgar cloud appears above
Minoress, projecting over the begonia. Minoress goes on untroubled,
but soon the obscure power of the cloud makes the begonia vanish
for good.

I willingly take my things and leave the villa with the logic that I'll
be able to express my opinion, until now only tangible in the ways I
styled my hair – the metaphors never took.

    I can't reverse the future.

Vile Minoress held the prophecies of our futures. Discrete
informations concerning everyone. In one vision she told me I had
wished her many happy returns.

A Course in Miracles

Sacred figures manifest for reasons that are often unclear
Such manifestations have been referred to before now
as avatars
Those who have received divine avatars
provide differing accounts which
like the pain of a headache
cannot be proven false
Records show the sacred
as having revealed themselves
at the sites of burning homes
and in the folds of discarded towels
with a similar frequency
though the most credited apparitions
have always occurred in groves
Early indicators
of forthcoming manifestations include
the sudden need to cover an object fully
with your hands
fierce attachment to a gift initially discarded
confusion of past and future events
disagreements about colour

. . .

Sometimes a divinity is more
than a mortal can stand
and he or she will burn
Sometimes earth tremors
and/or thunder and lightning
and/or smoke rising

will preface an appearance
Sometimes an appearance
relies on the complicity of clouds

. . .

The Saints

The saints see through roofs
and through the centuries
They see your thoughts
the future
your future thoughts
all of this at once
and from a great distance

You can't but imagine it
in terms of colour
perhaps a time-lapse sequence, fast heat

*
* *

The saints manifest in burning homes
The homes are their minds
but they're also real homes
Love is air (worthless)
Consciousness
consciousness is just the idea
that keeps you here

*
* *

The saints cause drama
dump cylinders
whumping cylinders by the ditch

Death Pact

Jessica's a fabulist
I tossed a carrot on the decking
He eats the bread like a sandwich
with no filling
Breakfast is for winners, she said
If it jars you then good
Brooms are the most sombre of the cleaning
tool family
Antonella is a fabulist
How often do you speak to yours?

Ed

Ed could see other people's headaches rising like heat haze
Grading papers she thought, 'An era cannot be *self-styled*'
Someone crunched up the gravel of her mind
glimpsed stone lions there on plinths, &
in plain view
turned back round

*
* *

Cropped gelled hair like a boy's
& an adolescent boy's pitch-dark nostrils
late afternoons Ed sets aside marking
attends to her speculative novel-in-progress*

*
* *

November, &
a PDF on translation & globalisation
finally relieved of its duty

---

* *On Gravity –*

. . . Her mother had died seven years ago. Anna had been sixty-two. She had never known her father, never had a step.

Anna's husband was her father. He frowned when she tripped over things, which happened increasingly frequently. Their marriage had taken place three weeks before Anna's twenty-third birthday.

Today Anna had tripped over the floor divider between kitchen and living room. She had moved herself onto the nearest sofa, gripping her foot in silence. Her husband hadn't looked. He had continued reading, but made sure to broadcast his exasperation for the invisible audience of their marriage with a grimace. He was seven years older than Anna.

Anna's husband was her brother. They would smack each other on the arms and torso, and playfight when there was a good mood. They mocked each other when one of them lost face, whether out in public or before the invisible audience of their marriage. Sometimes the mocking was taken with good grace, other times not.

Sometimes they loved each other. Sometimes they loved each other very much. Most often they loved each other very much after they had endured a period of mutual animosity so wild that it had culminated in Anna plotting to leave, an activity that, far from signalling the end, had the effect of razing all negative feeling. Anna couldn't know, but her husband must have undergone a similar mental process at such times, because it was after this oblivion had been reached that they would finally commune and understand one another as vital.

The cycle had been disrupted by the tripping and the dropping, however; there was fresh tension, beyond the usual run of things.

A university friend Anna was no longer in touch with had once confided in her when they had been sharing a house in South East London at the end of the last century, telling Anna that she had been subject to the most distressing thing Anna had ever heard first-hand. One of the earliest symptoms of her friend's consequent trauma, as she had related it, was the sensation of having her arms pulled down, towards the ground, as though her wrists had been pitched to the Earth with taut guylines|

Bunny

Where did the dust come from
and how much of it do you have?
When and where did you first notice
the dust? Why didn't you act sooner?
Why don't you show me a sample.
Why don't you have a sample?
Why don't you take some responsibility?
For yourself, the dust? Personally
I've never suffered from or even seen
the dust. No one I know has reported issues.
These are facts. The difference between us
is the difference between facts
and lies. You tell lies. Not only do you lie
about the dust, but you lie about
or altogether conceal your reasons
for having fabricated such a complaint. Any reason
I can conceive of that might have prompted you
to fabricate such a complaint is unrelated
and, in any case, is of your own doing.
Have you considered the impact of your complaint
on the ones you love? I recommend you
write out your issues [with the dust] in a draft email
and then delete it.
You need to forget about the dust.
There's simply no alternative for you.
Do you want to lose your children? I met them earlier
in the foyer, if you remember, and they didn't
cough once. Don't blame the dust for your poor parenting;

the dust is not an autonomous entity. The dust appears
if anything, to be synonymous with your own
sense of guilt, and if that's true, then all is dust, these words, Bunny.

Autobiography

Everyone agreed the white lie was beautiful. She'd presented it to him in the kind of box that looked expensive in and of itself. Of course, he thought it was a feather plucked from the tail of a piebald peacock, because that's what he'd been told. All the same, he kept it permanently out of sight. He couldn't say why. But it stayed there, beautifully.

THE ENGINE CONTINUED

Small white monkeys stretch around in the dirt beneath a tree but do not get dirty. They pick themselves up and dash away across the concrete plane, bobbing out of sight. They are silent.

I see faces in objects so frequently. Is this empathy? A door handle, a gate, a bony rock, a refuse sack, a tree, a church, a glove, a button, an icon . . .

On an oriental lamp base a floral design becomes a kind of ugly peony bonnet baby, petulant and saccharine.

'Finally I'm happy,' I think. I eat some supplements, drink some coffee and for hours everything is interesting.

I take over two hundred photos on my phone. Everything is poetry. Everything is trompe l'œil.

I try to think objectively about the discrete elements required of a masterpiece. I become itchy. I fall asleep.

The following evening is my dinner with the curator. I wear a fresh white gown.

During le plat principal my left bell sleeve slides through a rich sauce as I reach for my glass, but when I retract it the sauce slides right off. I bother the sleeve edge with my fingers for the rest of the evening.

The white monkeys watch me from a pylon, far away.

The dinner is ultimately disappointing. I had nothing to say, barely knowing any of the names the curator mentioned, and, on the few occasions I purported to recognise one, further discussion revealed me to be inept. I feel terribly guilty after the drink wears off.

I remember at one point noticing in my behaviour that I was more or less pretending to be the curator's daughter.

The next day I am offered an interview with a contemporary art magazine. I accept the invitation, and they never email again.

I wake up a day not long after, covered in milk. My nipples are leaking warm stuff all over. I get up and notice that I am pregnant; my belly is huge.

I update my social media profiles with the news. The curator stops contacting me. The editors stop contacting me. Only one or two of my peers continue to send me emails, and they have so little to say. They ask for updates on me and the pregnancy but the interest is all feigned. I cry and smoke packets of white cigarettes and don't tell anyone.

I tell everyone I'm not pregnant anymore. They have even less to say to me. Soon, I have a baby.

*
* *

After a declaration of interest I wait thirty-two months before I am invited to attend my pre-appointment at the Tropical Midnight Society. I locate the address provided in the email and arrive as instructed: freshly bathed with clean hair; dark, breathable clothes; no make-up make-up.

The chorus welcome me into a subterranean car park, dimly lit. They ask my name (Claudia Pulchra), and I tell them (Claudia Pulchra).

The air is thick and busy with incense. Members on the outer edge of the chorus are swinging single-chain thuribles. Electricity bursts like water from tubes in the exposed ceiling above us. We are surrounded by customised vehicles.

I am asked to give details pertaining to my application. I tell the chorus that I have information to ruin a man. The Meister distributes a set of photocopies.

As the chorus study the handout, I glimpse a figure escape through a side door, and next to the door a heap of snakes with snake eggs.

The photocopies show a series of photographs of small green-yellow bruises.

I am asked to create a password, after which I am no longer permitted to look the Meister in the eye.

I am led into an adjoining room where I must wait for a period. I fall asleep against an industrial appliance, and when I awake a woman with sympathies has appeared.

I put my hand in my pocket and thumb the lion's head of my inner resources before my clothes are taken from me.

When the initiation comes it is brutal and quick. As we approach the climax I seek out my reflection. I find it in the windows of a souped-up electric-blue car. I see that I am wet with sweat, a whole piece of skin has come away from my hairline, my lips are puckered and shining.

Suddenly I can smell myself, my armpits like hot squealing oil. I hear the vehicles rev their engines in tandem as black oil streams down my inner thighs.

A voice (my own?) calls me. I tread up to the steel pulpit like the sphinx that I am (bottom heavy). The Meister hands me a triangular white mouth covering to wear, and I take it and turn it upside down, and wear it as a crown.

Anna Karenina

Everyone has a future
but some have more than others

Lucia has made seven for herself
pails full of oil
all dark and density and difficult
for a girl to carry
with two arms and a yoke

Auntie says do not worry so
much over your future
but my future
– there is only one –
my future has heard this
and is become loud

A WHISTLE IN THE GLOOM

The feeling of inauthenticity under certain linguistic circumstances, of not being able to tell the truth, however strenuously one struggles to reach it – isn't this feeling commoner than is usually acknowledged?

. . .

The very grammar of the language of self-reference seems to demand, indeed to guarantee, an authenticity closely tied to originality. Yet simultaneously it cancels this possibility. Any I seems to speak for and from herself; her utterance comes from her own mouth in the first person pronoun which is hers, if only for just so long as she pronounces it. Yet as a human speaker, she knows that it's also everyone's, and that this grammatical offer of uniqueness is untrue, always snatched away.

. . .

My autobiography always arrives from somewhere outside me; my narrating I is really anybody's, promiscuously. Never mind the coming story of my life; simply to enunciate that initial 'I' makes me slow down in confusion.

Pauline Réage's *Story of O* follows the title character as she submits herself to the sexual predilections of a secret society. At the novel's outset, O's lover, René, takes her to a château on the outskirts of Paris where she is trained to serve the society's associates. O is flayed. She is manhandled and chained to the château's walls for hours at a time. She is instructed on matters pertaining to the society's sartorial customs and preferences. She is penetrated by one man after another in regular orgiastic sessions. René looks on. During one such session, an associate has difficulty entering O and demands that she have her anus stretched, which she does (after René approves the modification), in increments.

Subsequent trials follow at various locations as René's initial owner-ship of O is passed on to one man after another. O's second owner, Sir Stephen, has one of her labia pierced and adorned with a series of rings that form a heavy chain. To the heavy chain is attached a small disc engraved with a motif that signifies O's subjugation.

O consents to everything.

My own copy of Réage's text, a cracked black paperback with a spare, whitish font that dubs her novel 'The Erotic Classic', offers readers two distinct endings.

In the first, O, wearing nothing but a highly realistic bird mask, is led into a ball where she is made a strange attraction for its guests. Two children, a boy and a girl, are among those who engage with O. The boy forces the girl, who is wearing a white dress (indicating that this is her first ball), to sit down next to O and touch her breasts, to run her hand over O's labia, her piercing, its chain and tag. The young girl complies in silence, and then listens in silence as the boy tells her how, one day in the very near future, he will have the same thing done to her. Once the ball's attendants disperse, O is led to a stone platform where she is once again penetrated by multiple men.

In the second, alternative ending, O kills herself (or asks to be killed) when Sir Stephen makes clear his intention to relinquish her.

'Pauline Réage' was a pseudonym for Dominique Aury, a journalist, translator and editor at renowned literary publishers Gallimard. When she was willingly 'unmasked' in an article in the *New Yorker*, in 1994 (fifty years after *Story of O*'s initial publication in France), the disparity between the book's author – Aury's professional, public persona – and Réage's narrative (its sadomasochistic content) was relayed in tones of surprise.

In the article, Aury relates having started writing the book hotly and privately, at night, in bed, for her lover, Jean Paulhan, in an effort to revive what she perceived to be his waning interest.

Already a well-known intellectual and Aury's superior at Gallimard, Paulhan saw to it that *Story of O* was published and tried to improve its chances of commercial success by contributing a preface. In this text, titled 'A Slave's Revolt', Paulhan professes again and again his ignorance of the true author of the book, stating that the manuscript has the look 'of a letter more than of a diary'. 'But to whom is the letter addressed?', he writes. 'And whom does the discourse aim to convince? Whom is one to ask? I don't even know who you are.'

Aury was herself not sure. Asked about the book's sex scenes, she was adamant that the fantasies were neither her own nor something that, in the end, she particularly imagined would stimulate Paulhan, but belonged to an entity whose origins and shape she could not trace. 'I saw, between what I thought myself to be and what I was relating and thought I was making up, both a distance so radical and a kinship so profound that I was incapable of recognising myself in it,' she explained. 'I no doubt accepted my life with such patience (or passivity, or weakness) only because I was so certain of being able to find whenever I wanted that other obscure life that is life's consolation . . .'

Of the 'childish' chains and whips she said, 'All I know is that they were beneficent and protected me mysteriously.'

In a reading of Réage's text, the symbolism of O is impossible to resist, despite the author's consistent attestations as to the letter's arbitrary nature.

Here I will purge the associations by listing them: zero (none); an exclamation (archaic); a lament (archaic); an interjection (archaic); a circle; a ring; any body orifice, including a gasping mouth or gaping anus; and, more tenuously, the grand rooms and dungeons to whose walls O is fixed; a mirror; an eye; a wound.

O was originally named after a friend of Réage's, Odile (a moniker shared by Pyotr Tchaikovsky's Black Swan and Odile of Alsace, patron saint of good eyesight). Shortly, however, Réage found herself unable to project O's experiences onto Odile, and so erased the majority of the name, rendering her protagonist an initial – a conspicuous lack.

'Initial', from the Latin for 'standing at the beginning'.

At the beginning of the book, O is not standing but sitting, in a car (a cab), her skirt gathered up in order to allow her bare genitals to rest directly on the vehicle's leather upholstery.

Before I know the details of its origins, *Story of O* is a book I treat as an artefact, a ruin I explore for its beauty, its strangeness, its shattered intimidations; I rub my open palms across its scaly parapets while looking out at the developing world I usually inhabit.

During one such visit, *O* seems to effect its own modality, to constitute a part of speech other than its designation as a proper noun.

'O heard a whistle in the gloom',

'O placed a new log on the fire',

'O listened and trembled from happiness' –

I type out these disembodied phrases and read them again and again until, whimsically, and for moments at a time, I allow myself to comprehend *O* not as an initial, but as a personal pronoun; a Rubenesque alternative to *I*; an innovation in grammar signifying a tacit acknowledgement of the paradoxes of self-expression; a room to live and breathe in, with some honesty.

I recently read, in another poet's poem, a passage that claimed apparently impersonal poems as the by-products of trauma.

I witnessed, noiselessly, a thought forming; I watched it take shape as one watches a small movement in the distance: with a fleeting sense of calm.

I read the passage again, and I understood it. I understood it, and I felt the shame rise; I knew that the poet was right; I knew that she was absolutely wrong.

Creating isn't imagination, it's taking the great risk of grasping reality.

A.S.

And what was it Anna Sofia couldn't say? That all had started with Arlo, when she had started up with Arlo, who had been nice enough, but whose presence had turned her into herself. And so first the faces, then mainly the eyes, but, in the end, all of it really.

And what was it she couldn't say she was after? To smash to pieces the earthenware jug on the stove top? The sound of a veil tearing? Both were nice ideas, but she couldn't stick with them. She walked around a bit and started to blurt things out. She told old men just how much they smelled, that their breath smelled and more, and this got her into some real trouble. A white old man, pale lizard face, small teeth, paper neck, hat the colour of yellow dog shit . . .

He came at her in an alleyway with the red tie just as bad, and, quick as she needed to be, A.S. had pulled out a razor knife – could have been Arlo's, could have been anyone's – and flicked it at his papery neck.

She would tell them she had been where she had always intended to be that day in September 2013: the Mushrooms and Health Summit, Washington, D.C. And if it didn't get her off (it wouldn't), it didn't matter. Powerful, she can cook.

Ed

She knew nothing; no language, no history

Her hair smelled of whisky
from the night before

POSTFACE

The author receives an email from a press that wishes to
    publish her first book.
She signs a contract.
She moves countries.
The author has trouble focusing and is always thirsty.
She is experiencing a poor quality of life, emotionally speaking.
She wishes to quit her body.
The author receives an email inviting her to interview for a
    full-time academic position.
She receives an email requesting a face-to-face meeting to
    discuss a residency application.
She attends the interview.
The author attends the face-to-face meeting.
She accepts the residency.
She regretfully declines the full-time academic position.

The author pulls some boxes from an archive.

She opens a box marked VIOLENCE AGAINST WOMEN BOX 5.

She reads a short text on the use of lemon juice as an offensive
weapon.

The author opens a box marked VIOLENCE AGAINST WOMEN
BOX 4.

She sifts newspaper clippings.

She takes photographs.

The author tells those who ask that she is undertaking a residency.

She tells those who show interest that she is thinking about shame.

She is asked on more than one occasion to offer a distinction
between shame and guilt.

The author joins a copyright library.

She reads parts of Sara Ahmed's *The Cultural Politics of Emotion*.

She transcribes, *In shame, I am the object as well as the subject of
the feeling.*

The author enjoys a renewed sense of the mind's ductility.

She works on her book.

She notices that she no longer wishes to quit her body as such.

The author reads parts of Sandra Lee Bartky's *Femininity and Domination*.

She reads, *shame requires if not an actual audience before whom my deficiencies are paraded, then an internalised audience with the capacity to judge me.*

She feels seen, in some important sense.

The author receives an email inviting her to read at a gallery.

She accepts the invitation.

She casually teaches poetics to undergraduates.

The author wakes up early on the day of the reading.

She prints new work.

She travels south.

Note on Fan Fiction

Fan fiction is writing that appropriates existing texts by adopting the characters and/or settings of published fiction. It is usually unauthorised, uncommissioned work created by fans of the source text. Subgenres of fan fic include 'curtain fic', in which characters in an ongoing romantic relationship engage in casual domestic activities such as cooking or doing the laundry (or selecting new curtains), and 'Hurt/Comfort', in which the fan fic author inflicts emotional or physical harm on one character in order to have them be subsequently comforted by another.

An oft-cited and early example of fan fic is Jean Rhys's 1966 novel *Wide Sargasso Sea*, a prequel of sorts to Charlotte Brontë's *Jane Eyre* (1847). Rhys was not a fan of *Jane Eyre*, but of the book's Creole spectre, Bertha Antoinetta Mason. Portrayed as the violently insane first wife of Jane Eyre's love interest, Mr Rochester, Mason is famously locked in the attic of her husband's home. On escaping, Mason sets the building alight, definitively burning it down (she has set smaller fires before) and blinding Rochester in the process. In a letter to a female friend, Rhys wrote of her novel, 'I think of calling it "*The first Mrs Rochester*" with profound apologies to Charlotte Brontë and a deep curtsey too. But I suppose that won't do (I'm supposing you've studied Jane Eyre like a good girl).' *Wide Sargasso Sea* establishes an origin story for Bertha Mason, or Antoinette Cosway, as Rhys renames her.

Speaking of the book, Rhys's editor, Diana Athill, wrote that, having moved from Dominica at sixteen, Rhys hated England and the English 'for despising (as she was sure they did) her ignorance and her home . . . I saw it flare up when a woman spoke of Castries, in St. Lucia, as "a shanty town" . . . *Wide Sargasso Sea* was inspired by this hate'.

Other Notes

The epigraph to this book comes from a collage by French artist and writer Claude Cahun, as featured in *Disavowals; or Cancelled Confessions* (the translation is mine).

In the Preface ('I recently read . . .'), italicised phrases come from Rachel Cusk's *The Last Supper* and an interview with Kim Hyesoon conducted in Korean by Yi Ŭn-kyu and Kwon Hyôk-ung, and translated into English by Don Mee Choi.

The image that follows is a photo of Euterpe taken and sent to me by Emily Berry.

'Sister' and 'Untitled' came out of deviant translations made as part of a collaboration with Polish poet Małgosia Lebda.

In 'Who Is Mary Sue?', quotes are taken from, in the following order: Camille Bacon-Smith's *Enterprising Women*; Joanna Russ's *How to Suppress Women's Writing*; an interview with Lorrie Moore, 'The Art of Fiction No. 167', in *The Paris Review*; a filmed interview with Jamaica Kincaid for *TIME*, available on YouTube; an interview with Lucy Ives conducted by Kendra Sullivan in *BOMB Magazine*; an interview with Sharon Olds first published in *Poets & Writers Magazine* (and now available in excerpted form on the *Modern American Poetry* website); and an interview with Rachel Cusk, 'Medea is about divorce . . . A couple fighting is an eternal predicament. Love turning to hate', as featured in the *Guardian*.

The epigraph to 'The Engine' is from an interview with Barbara T. Smith in *BOMB Magazine*, conducted by Mary Jones.

The italicised text at the beginning of 'a whistle in the gloom' is excerpted from Denise Riley's *The Words of Selves*. The final sentence is from Idra Novey's translation of Clarice Lispector, *The Passion According to G.H.*

Dominique Aury was also a pseudonym, chosen for its gender neutrality. Aury's given name is stated elsewhere; I won't use it here.

My edition of *Story of O* does not credit a translator.

Borrowed and/or generative lines: in 'a whistle in the gloom', the phrase 'its beauty, its strangeness, its shattered intimidations' is borrowed from Rose Macaulay's *Pleasure of Ruins*; the latter 'Ed' begins with a line ('She knew nothing . . .') from Virginia Woolf's *Mrs Dalloway*.

In 'Note on Fan Fiction', quotes are taken from Jean Rhys's *Letters, 1931–1966* and Diana Athill's *Stet*, respectively.

Acknowledgements

This book is for Sam, Shelly, Wilma, Rachael, Nora, Livia and Harriet.

Thank you to my parents, and to Lavinia, Jack, Eva, George, Emily, Daisy, Nuar and Tara.

Thank you to Grace Johnston, curator of *Ours* at Collective, Edinburgh, for commissioning '*a whistle in the gloom*'. Thank you to Laura McLean-Ferris, curator of *Columbidae* at Cell Project Space, London, for introducing me to Barbara T. Smith's *The Poetry Sets* and her life and other work.

Thank you to the following presses and journals in whose publications some of these poems first appeared: *Ambit*, *Blackbox Manifold*, *clinic*, *Five Dials*, *Ploughshares*, *Poetry*, *Poetry London*, *Powder Keg*, *The White Review*, *The Wolf*.

I am grateful to Arts Council England and Creative Scotland, who helped me financially at different stages.